AF405690

DIONYSUS: KILLED MANY TIMES, SURVIVED EVERY TIME

GREEK MYTHOLOGY FOR KIDS CHILDREN'S GREEK & ROMAN BOOK

Speedy Publishing LLC

40 E. Main St. #1156

Newark, DE 19711

www.speedypublishing.com

Copyright 2017

All Rights reserved. No part of this book may be reproduced or used in any way or form or by any means whether electronic or mechanical, this means that you cannot record or photocopy any material ideas or tips that are provided in this book.

In this book, we're going to talk about the Greek god Dionysus. So, let's get right to it!

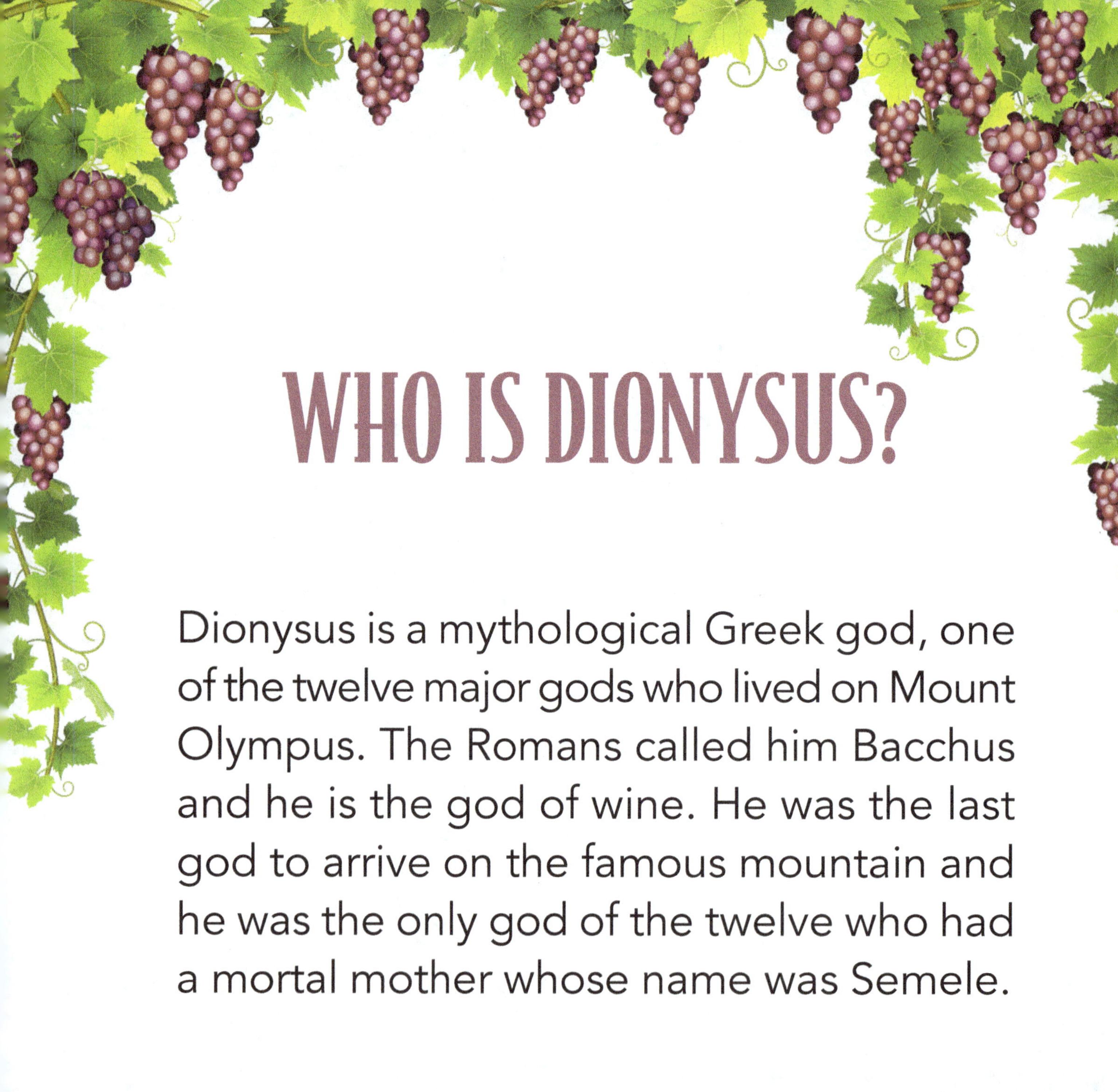

WHO IS DIONYSUS?

Dionysus is a mythological Greek god, one of the twelve major gods who lived on Mount Olympus. The Romans called him Bacchus and he is the god of wine. He was the last god to arrive on the famous mountain and he was the only god of the twelve who had a mortal mother whose name was Semele.

DIONYSUS

STATUE OF BACCHUS

The story of his parentage, birth, and death vary in different myths. One of the reasons for this is because Dionysus came from an earlier history than the Greeks.

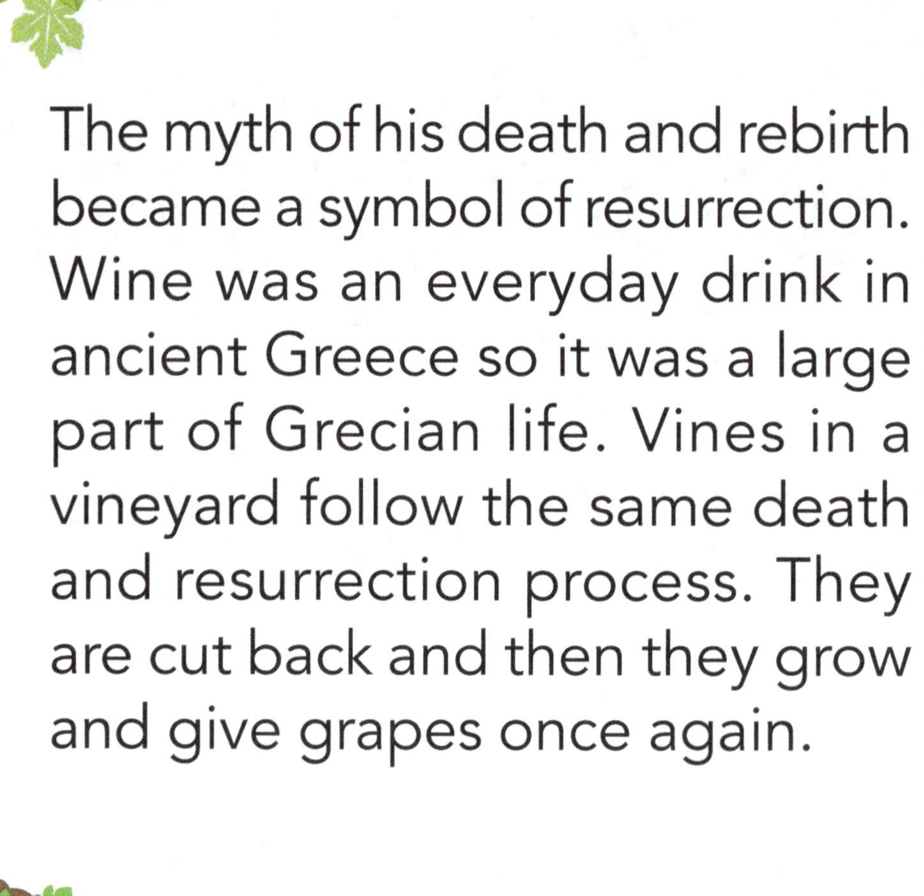

The myth of his death and rebirth became a symbol of resurrection. Wine was an everyday drink in ancient Greece so it was a large part of Grecian life. Vines in a vineyard follow the same death and resurrection process. They are cut back and then they grow and give grapes once again.

WINE

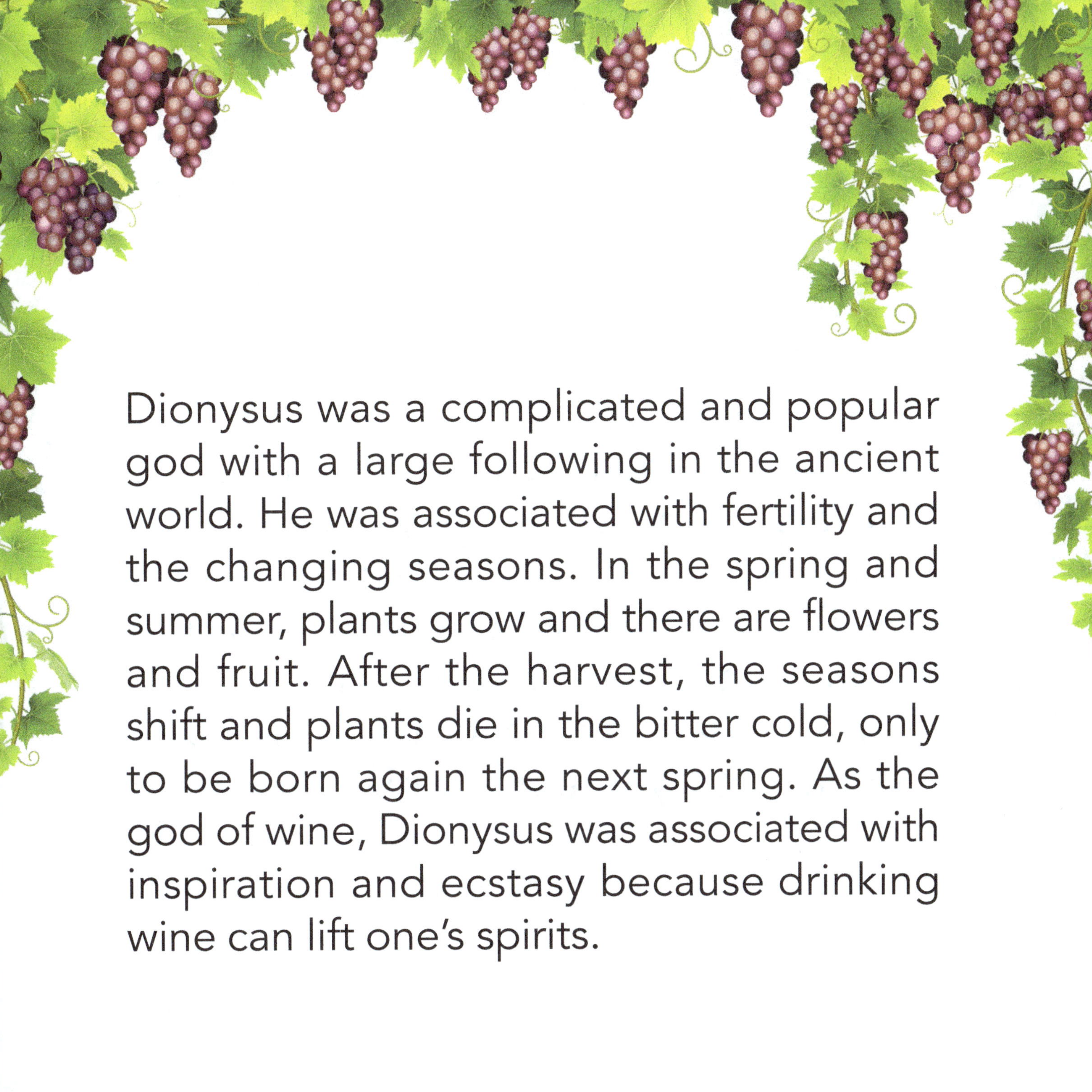

Dionysus was a complicated and popular god with a large following in the ancient world. He was associated with fertility and the changing seasons. In the spring and summer, plants grow and there are flowers and fruit. After the harvest, the seasons shift and plants die in the bitter cold, only to be born again the next spring. As the god of wine, Dionysus was associated with inspiration and ecstasy because drinking wine can lift one's spirits.

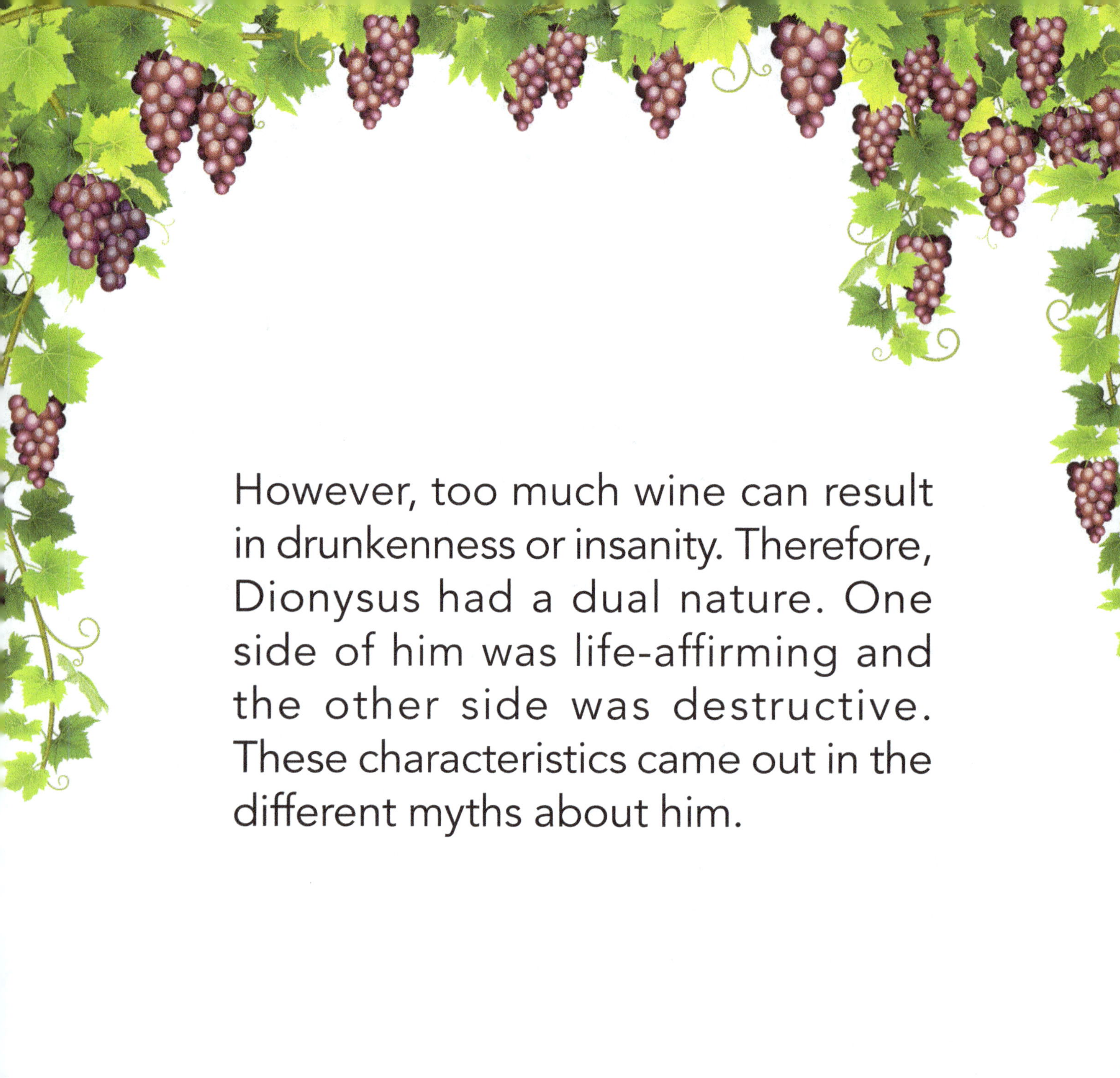

However, too much wine can result in drunkenness or insanity. Therefore, Dionysus had a dual nature. One side of him was life-affirming and the other side was destructive. These characteristics came out in the different myths about him.

THE BACKGROUND AND ORIGINS OF DIONYSUS

Dionysus didn't start out as a Greek god. He was first worshipped in Thrace, a region located north of Greece, as well as in Phrygia, which is now known as modern Turkey. His followers would get drunk, and then have wild rituals, so, at the beginning, the Greeks didn't worship him.

ANCIENT RUINS OF PHRYGIA, TURKEY

When his cult followers arrived in Rome, they kept their ceremonies secret. Eventually, both the Greeks and the Romans became followers of Dionysus.

ANCIENT ROMAN FRESCO SHOWING A DETAIL OF THE
MYSTERY CULT OF DIONYSUS

BACCHUS

HOW WAS DIONYSUS DEPICTED?

In most Greek art and sculpture, Dionysus is depicted as a young man with long unruly locks, but unlike other gods, he doesn't look athletic or strong. His head was often crowned with ivy and he wore the skins of animals or robes the color of deep purple grapes.

The staff he carried, which was called a thyrsus, had a pine cone, a symbol of fertility. The magical wine goblet that he held could fill up with wine on its own.

ZEUS

THE THEME OF DYING AND REBIRTH

There are many myths that involve Dionysus, but one of the myths that was frequently told was the story of his birth. Zeus was the king of all the gods and his wife was the goddess Hera. Zeus had other romantic partners besides his wife and Hera was very jealous of these other women, both goddesses and mortals.

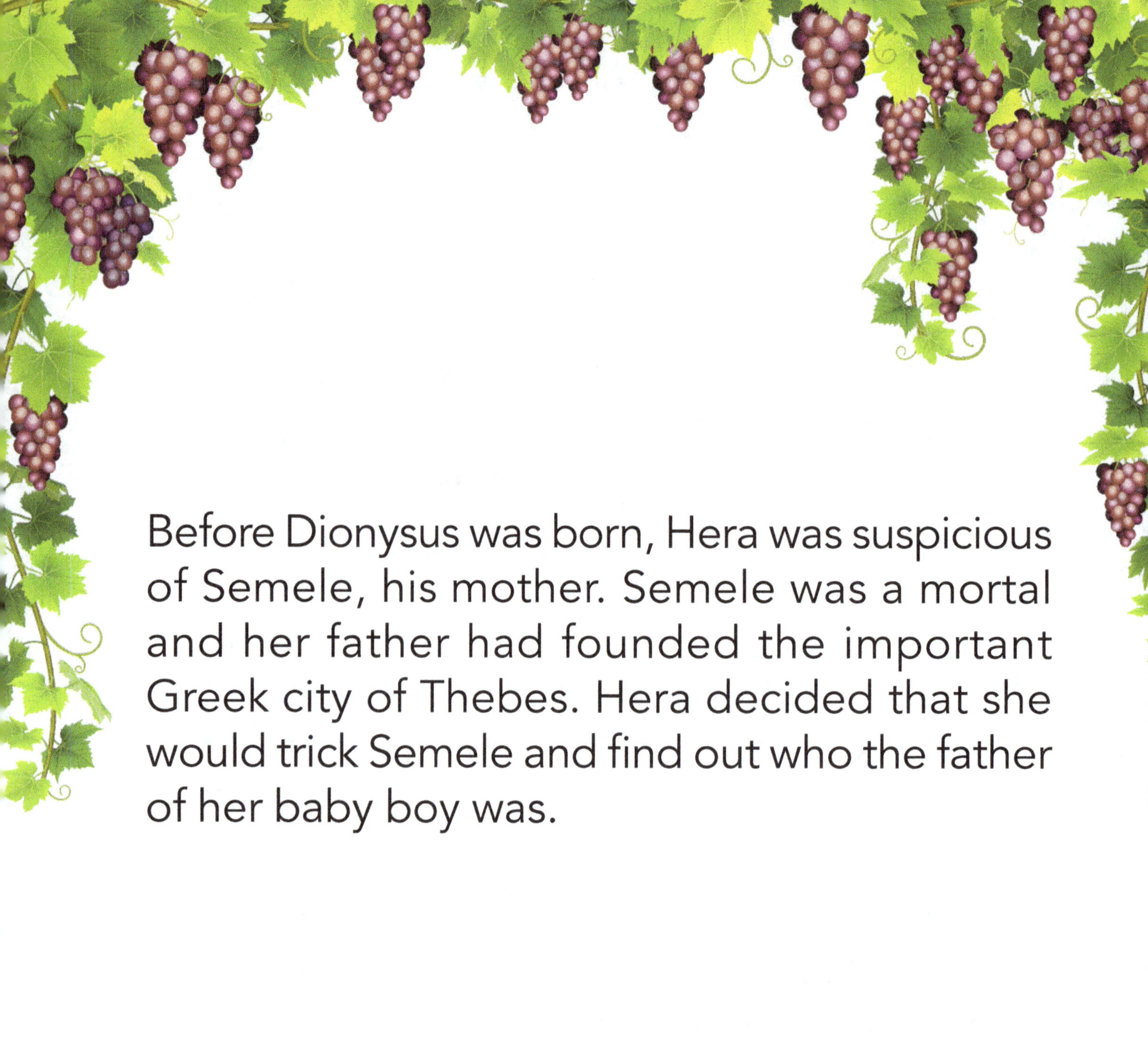

Before Dionysus was born, Hera was suspicious of Semele, his mother. Semele was a mortal and her father had founded the important Greek city of Thebes. Hera decided that she would trick Semele and find out who the father of her baby boy was.

HERA

Hera changed herself into the old nurse who took care of Semele. She asked her who the father of her baby was. Semele told her that the baby's father was the god of all gods, Zeus. The old nurse, who was really Hera in disguise, told Semele that she didn't believe her and wanted her to prove that her story was true.

Of course, Hera knew that if Semele saw Zeus she would die, because he was the god of powerful lightning. Semele called upon Zeus to show himself and when he did show his face, she died because she was turned to ashes by a bolt of lightning. However, Zeus knew what was going on, because Hera was forever causing him trouble. He took Dionysus from Semele's womb right before she died and placed the child inside his cut-open thigh.

INO AND HER HUSBAND, ATHAMAS

A season later, Dionysus was born from Zeus's thigh. When Hera found out that the child that Zeus had had with Semele had survived, she was furious and vowed to do injury to the child and his family. Semele's sister, who was named Ino, and her husband were taking care of baby Dionysus. Ino dressed the baby as a girl so Hera couldn't find him. However, the clever and ruthless Hera found out about the child and she punished his adoptive parents by driving them both insane.

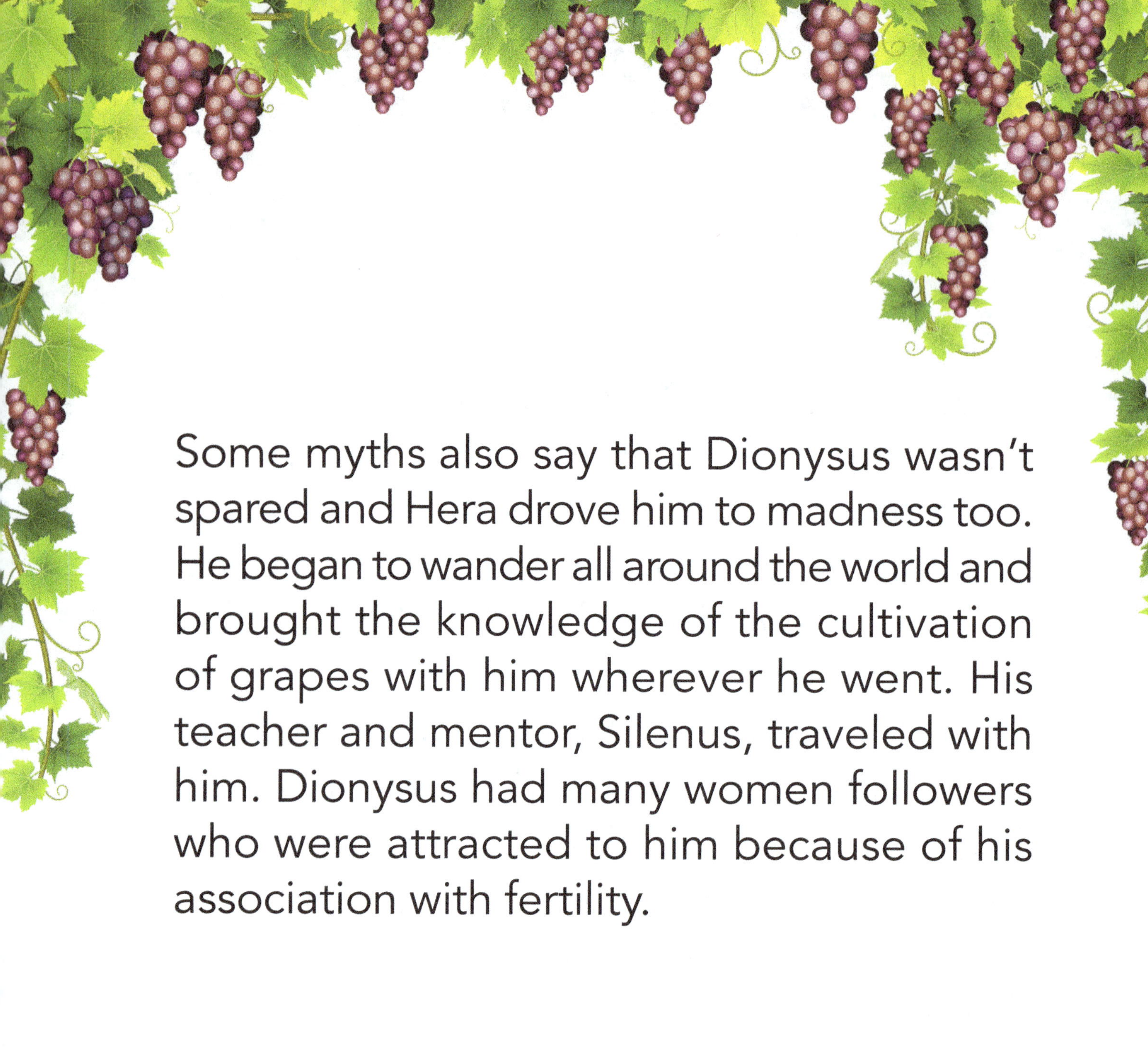

Some myths also say that Dionysus wasn't spared and Hera drove him to madness too. He began to wander all around the world and brought the knowledge of the cultivation of grapes with him wherever he went. His teacher and mentor, Silenus, traveled with him. Dionysus had many women followers who were attracted to him because of his association with fertility.

SILENUS

STATUES OF SATYRS

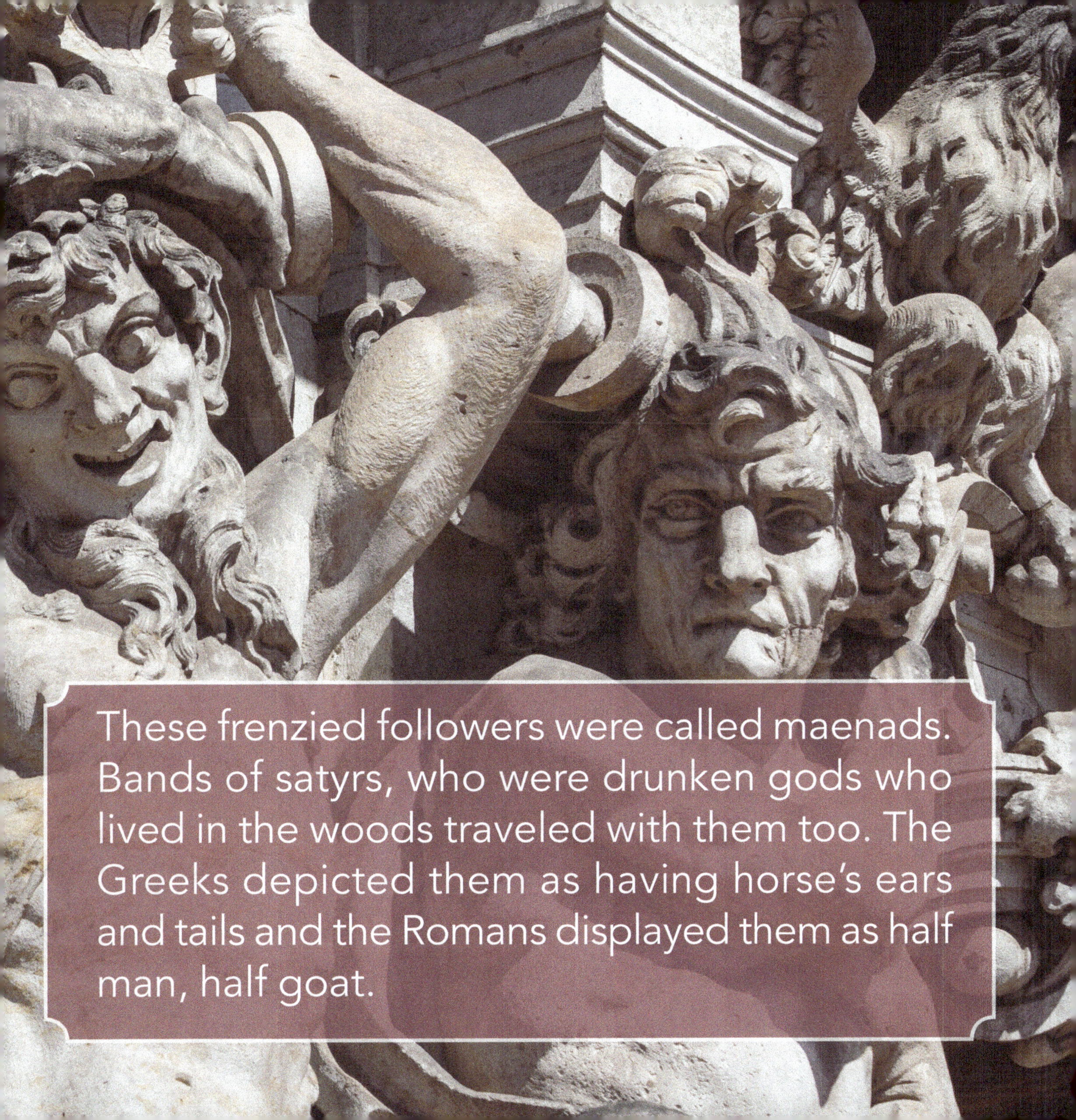

These frenzied followers were called maenads. Bands of satyrs, who were drunken gods who lived in the woods traveled with them too. The Greeks depicted them as having horse's ears and tails and the Romans displayed them as half man, half goat.

Of the many gods, Dionysus traveled the most. In Egypt, he taught the people how to cultivate grapes and make wine. He set up an oracle, an individual who was able to foretell the future, in the desert of the country of Libya. In India, he was known for establishing laws, building cities, and bringing the love of wine as he traveled and conquered all those who tried to stop him.

TEMPLE OF DIONYSUS

As Dionysus returned to Greece, he met Cybele along the way. She was his grandmother and the goddess of the Earth. She healed him so he was no longer insane and she taught him the secrets of the cycle of life and rebirth.

This myth about Dionysus contains three important themes: hostility, madness, and resurrection.

STATUE OF CYBELE

Dionysus and his followers encounter hostility wherever they go. He first faces the wrath of Hera and later must fight the resistance and hostility of the populations in the countries where he travels.

MOSAIC, DIONYSUS PARTY

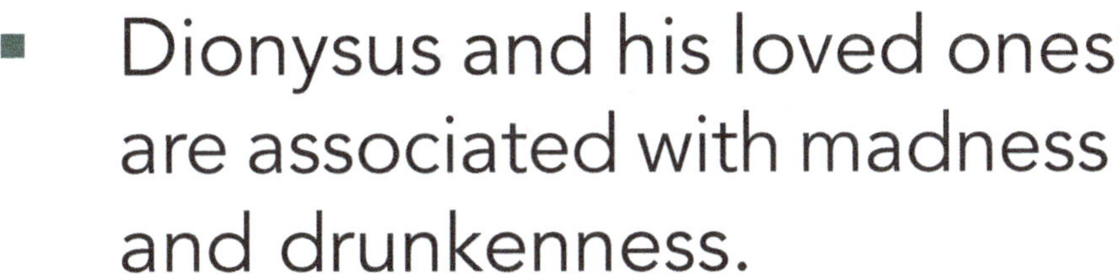

- Dionysus and his loved ones are associated with madness and drunkenness.

- Dionysus dies and is born again many times, just like the Earth's seasons.

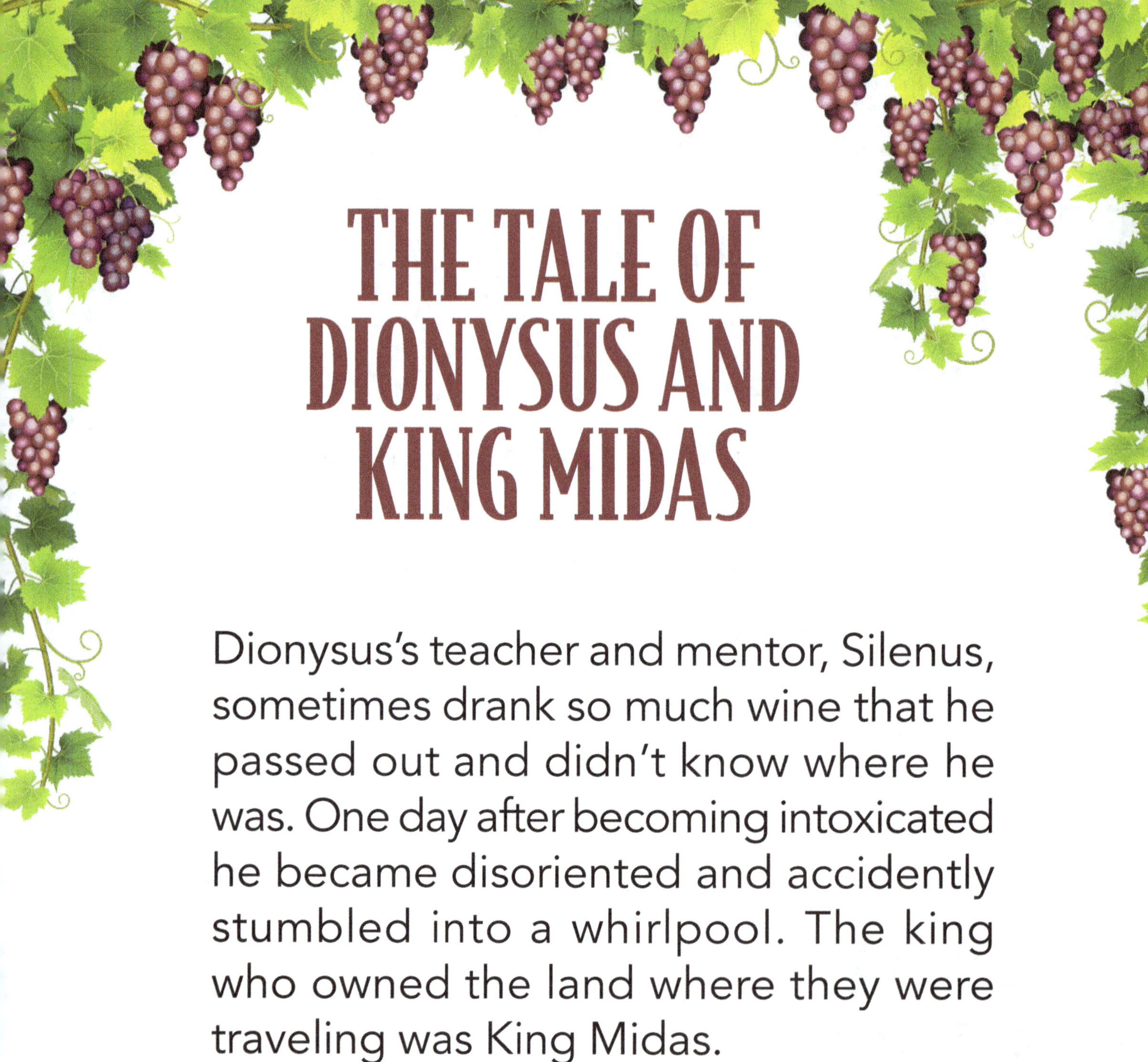

THE TALE OF DIONYSUS AND KING MIDAS

Dionysus's teacher and mentor, Silenus, sometimes drank so much wine that he passed out and didn't know where he was. One day after becoming intoxicated he became disoriented and accidently stumbled into a whirlpool. The king who owned the land where they were traveling was King Midas.

KING MIDAS

He saw Silenus fall and saved him from the swirling waters. As a reward for saving his teacher, Dionysus granted King Midas a wish. Midas wished that when he touched anything that it would turn into true gold.

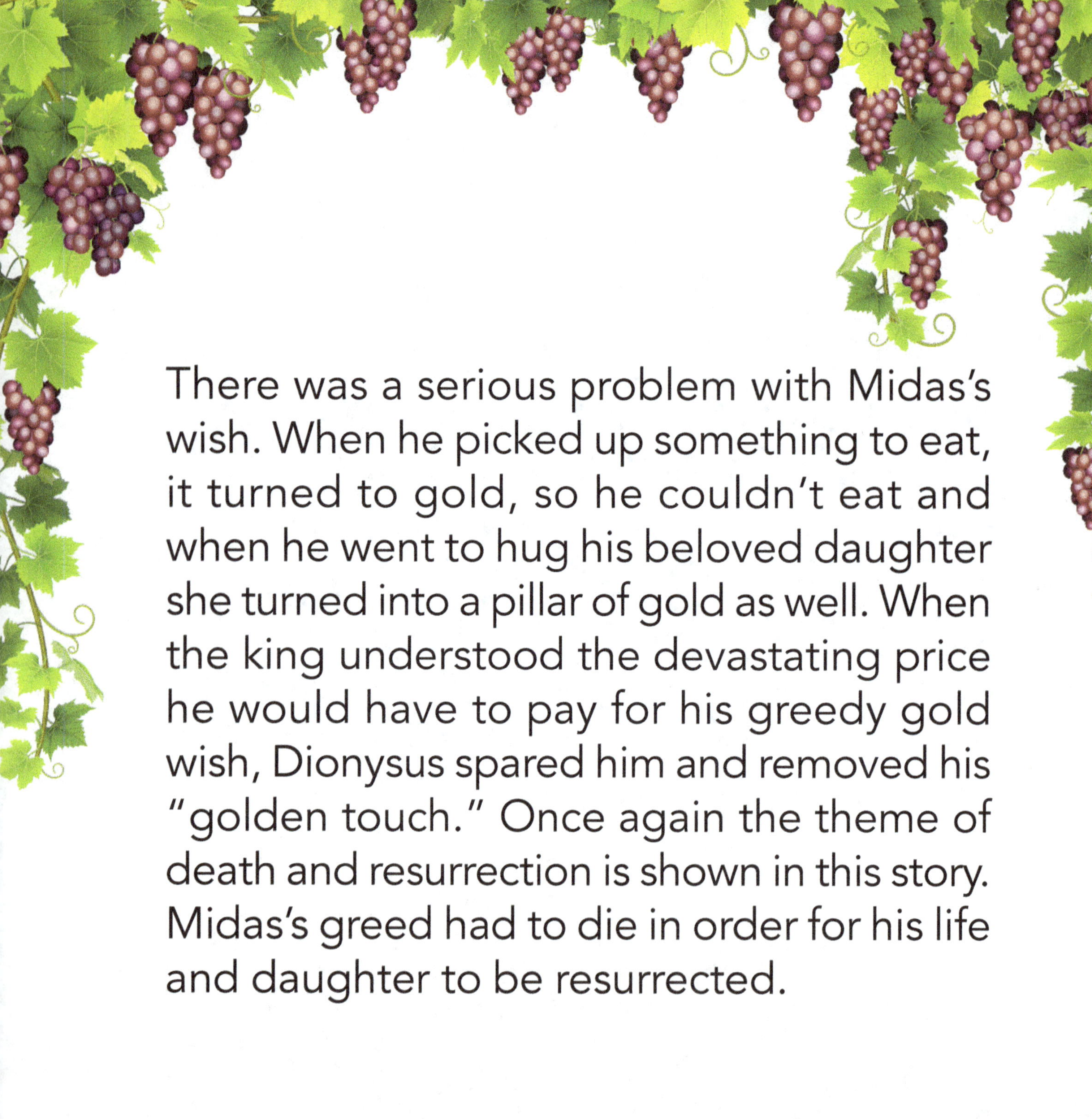

There was a serious problem with Midas's wish. When he picked up something to eat, it turned to gold, so he couldn't eat and when he went to hug his beloved daughter she turned into a pillar of gold as well. When the king understood the devastating price he would have to pay for his greedy gold wish, Dionysus spared him and removed his "golden touch." Once again the theme of death and resurrection is shown in this story. Midas's greed had to die in order for his life and daughter to be resurrected.

DEMETER

AN ALTERNATE STORY OF DIONYSUS'S BIRTH

As with many Greek and Roman myths, there are often alternate stories and Dionysus has another story about his birth. In this story, which is quite gruesome, his parents are Zeus and Demeter. Demeter is the goddess of vegetation and crops. Once again the jealous and destructive Hera intervened.

Furious that Zeus had been unfaithful with the goddess Demeter, Hera persuaded the Titans, a race of strong giants, to destroy the baby.

Even though Dionysus had been transformed into a young goat to keep his identity secret, the Titans found him and they tore him to shreds. They consumed his body with the exception of his heart, which was discovered and rescued by the goddess Athena.

Athena brought the heart back to Zeus and he gave it to the mortal Semele. She ate Dionysus's heart and then later gave birth to Dionysus. This story has a hidden meaning. Zeus represents the sky and Demeter represents the Earth. Their joining produces Dionysus, who represents crops. The crops and vegetation die every winter season and then are reborn in the spring. Dionysus died but was once again reborn.

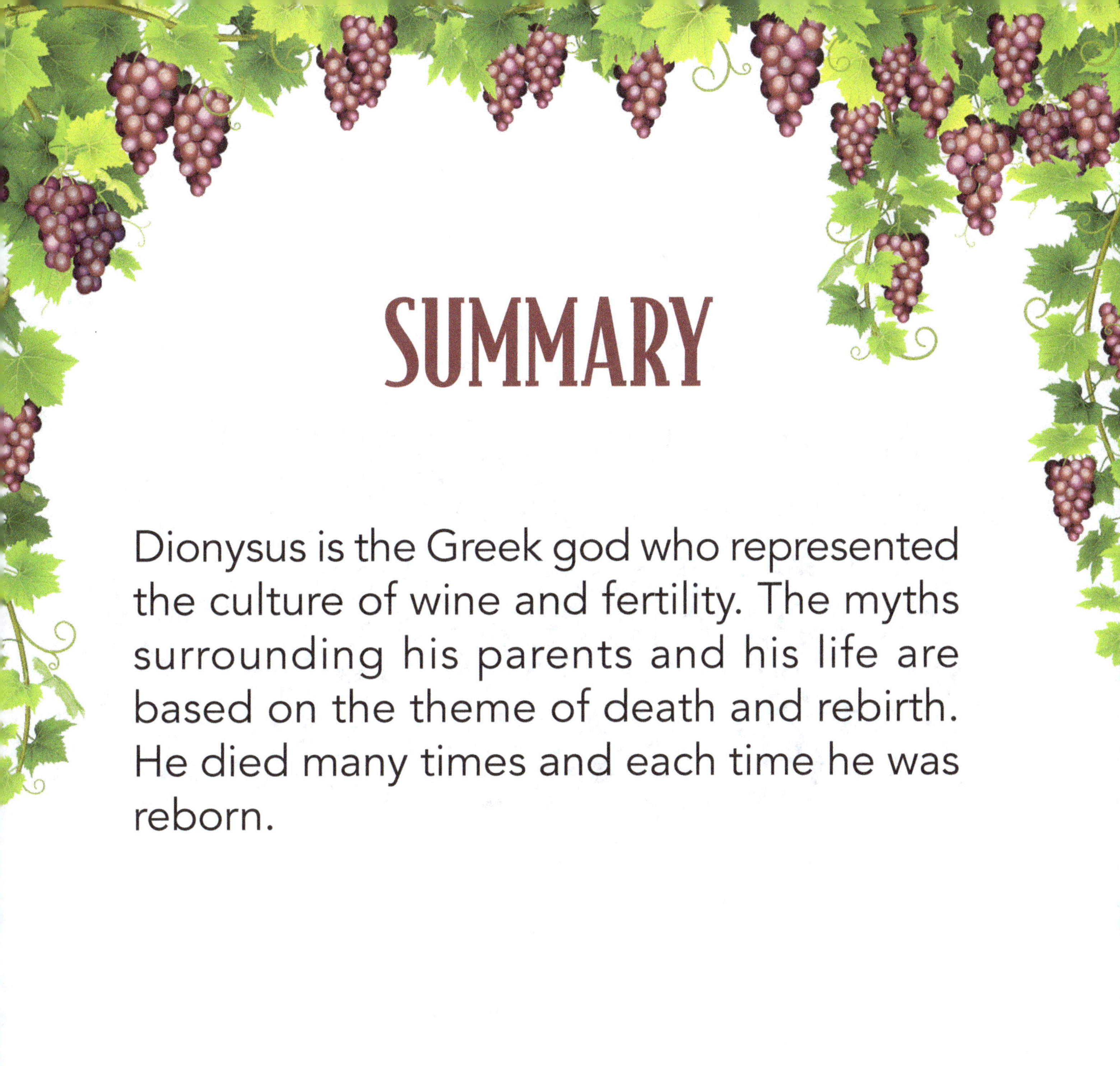

SUMMARY

Dionysus is the Greek god who represented the culture of wine and fertility. The myths surrounding his parents and his life are based on the theme of death and rebirth. He died many times and each time he was reborn.

Awesome! Now that you've read about the Greek god Dionysus, you may want to read about another Greek god in the Baby Professor book *Hades: The Only Olympian God Who Didn't Live on Mount Olympus – Greek Mythology for Kids.*

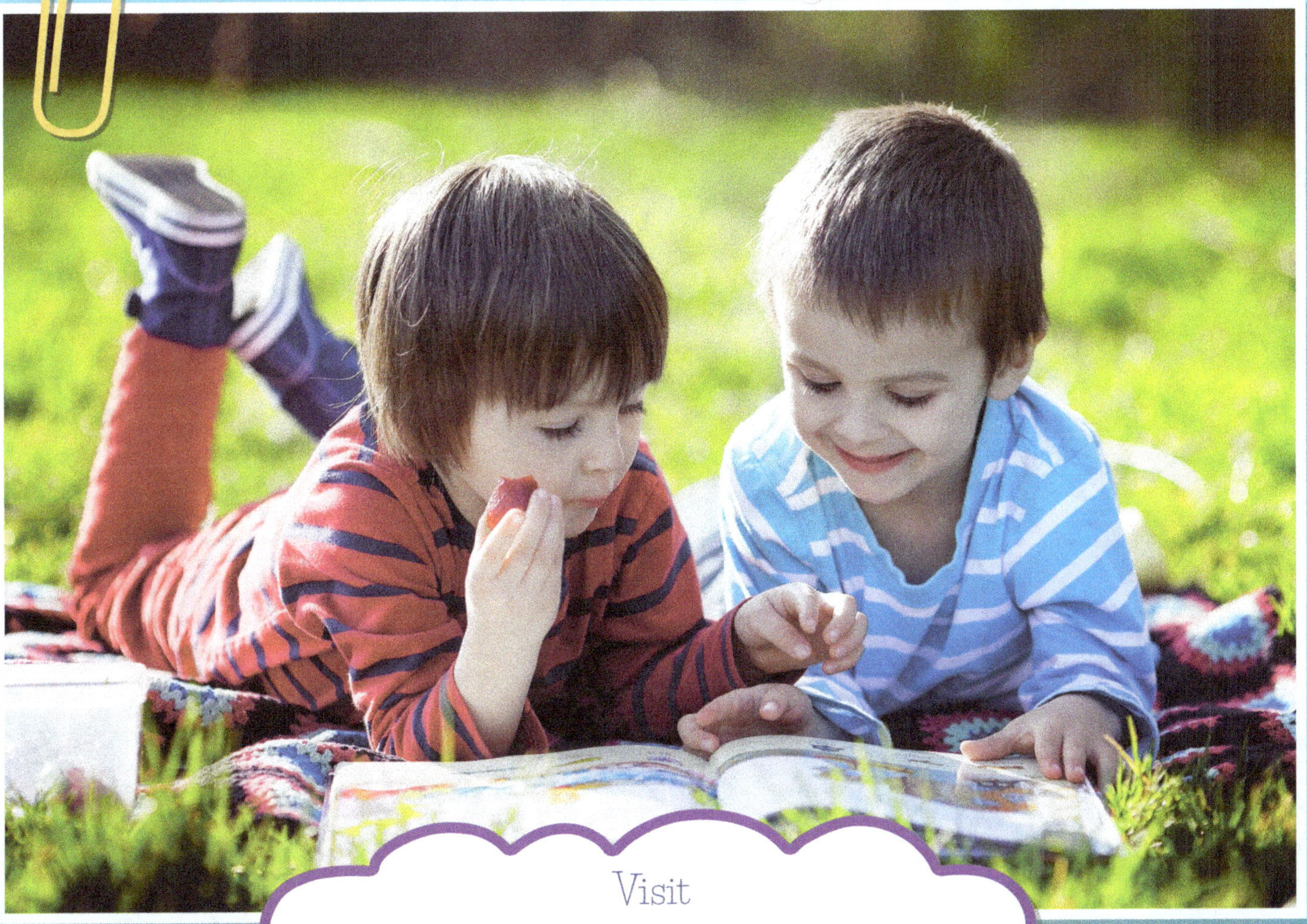

Visit

www.BabyProfessorBooks.com

to download Free Baby Professor eBooks
and view our catalog of new and exciting
Children's Books

www.ingramcontent.com/pod-product-compliance
Lightning Source LLC
Chambersburg PA
CBHW081231130726

47997CB00009B/2847